A moment of tranquility while reading April's poems is medicine. Her poems are invitations to reflection and creativity, embracing one's healing journey. Her poems foster and promote self-care and honor the wonderful feeling of just being in gratitude in life!

—Sonia Lucana, PhD (ancestral healing),
LCSW, RPT-S, hypnotherapist

In *The Garden Path to My Heart: Finding Inner Peace through Haiku*, April Joy Manger invites us into meditation through poetry on nature, daily life, and inner life. Sharing moments of joy, sorrow, alienation, and understanding, she leads us on a path through flowers' "scented abundance," asks us t[illegible] observe [illegible] watching [illegible] advises:

"Listen to silence
The sounds of everyday life
Hear the earth moving"

The haiku in *The Garden Path to My Heart* are touching, heartfelt, and often wise. The accompanying photographs are striking and thought-provoking. The poet writes to share her insights and move us toward more mindful and peaceful lives—a generous undertaking. Reading April Manger's writing, I find myself thinking it's no accident that her middle name is Joy.

—Elinor Gale, author of
The Emancipation of Emily Rosenbloom

The Garden Path to My Heart

FINDING INNER PEACE THROUGH HAIKU

April Joy Manger

ISBN: 978-1-7343786-0-3 (paperback)
ISBN: 978-1-7343786-1-0 (e-book)

Library of Congress Control Number: 2019920101

Copyediting, design, and production by Joanne Shwed, Backspace Ink (backspaceink.com)

Back cover photo by Suzanne Camac

projectgardengate.com
projectgardengate.com/blog

A percentage of the net profits will be contributed to my favorite nonprofit organizations.

My first book of poems is dedicated to my mother:

Ruth B. Manger

My mother is the bravest, most intelligent and loving person I have ever known.

I am eternally grateful to her for all the inspiration she gives me. She has encouraged me to pursue my love for writing poetry and motivated me to publish my first collection of poems.

From my heart, thank you, Mother!

ACKNOWLEDGEMENTS

My first book of poems would not have been possible without the professional copyediting and design expertise of Joanne Shwed with Backspace Ink. It was not a coincidence that I was guided to her.

I am extremely grateful to Ralph O. Sharp for his dedication to my purpose by spending countless hours working on the Project Garden Gate website. Ralph has supported my dream and was instrumental in making it a reality.

My deepest gratitude to my family and friends who give me moral and loving support to continue on my quest for inspiring others to follow their hearts, and to my friend Stephen, who challenged me to write from the depths of my heart and encouraged me to have my poems published. I would also like to thank my faithful and loyal website email subscribers.

Finally, my gratitude to Pixabay for making available copyright-free photographs by amazing and artistic photographers.

CONTENTS

CONTENTS

I love biting into a chunk of rich, dark chocolate, swirling it around my mouth as it slowly melts, while sipping a fine Pinot Noir before swallowing the satisfying blend of delicious flavors. The reading of haiku should be savored equally in this way, experiencing the breadth and depth of each poetic morsel.

April Joy Manger invites us into her private garden to share personal spaces with visions of color, light, and, of course, love that weaves it all together.

Her poems ring true to the format and spirit of Masaoka Shiki (1867–1902), a Japanese poet instrumental in the development of modern haiku. Influenced by the European Impressionists, who took their easels to the open air, Shiki adapted his writings to an approach he called shasei ("sketching from life").

The collection of poems in *The Garden Path to My Heart: Finding Inner Peace through Haiku*, illustrated by the added beauty of photography, walks us through highs and lows of human confrontations that surround and engage our daily lives. April finds a way, through each poem, to connect with the emotion of the moment, then visualize and grow from the experience.

—Thomas A. Ekkens,
Collected Poetry of Thomas A. Ekkens—Early Works

When I began writing haiku poetry seven years ago, my goal was to become more creative. As I tapped into the present moment, a new vision of the world gradually appeared around me—inspiring me to see beyond.

My favorite place to write is my living room, which has a large picture window with a peaceful and inspiring view. The first things I see are two beautiful weeping willow trees. Taking a closer look, long dangling branches gently sway in the breeze.

After I sit down and get comfortable, beauty begins to surface that I would have otherwise missed without taking the time to breathe and relax.

The longer I sit and observe, my connection to nature and to anything that is within my vision becomes stronger. I sense the energy of the wind between and around the tree branches and leaves, and over and under the wings of birds.

My window view gives me a front-row seat to magnificent sunsets with rays of love streaming through the window to my soul. A renewed connection to my environment emerges, and love is the resounding frequency.

Love has become my focus, and all I see is love—even in the sounds of a passing car or an airplane moving across the sky in my peripheral vision.

Writing haiku poetry has also become a way to ground and center myself—breathing and letting go of whatever stress I may have experienced during the day.

Seeing love in everything may be one of the secrets to living to a happier and more peaceful life.

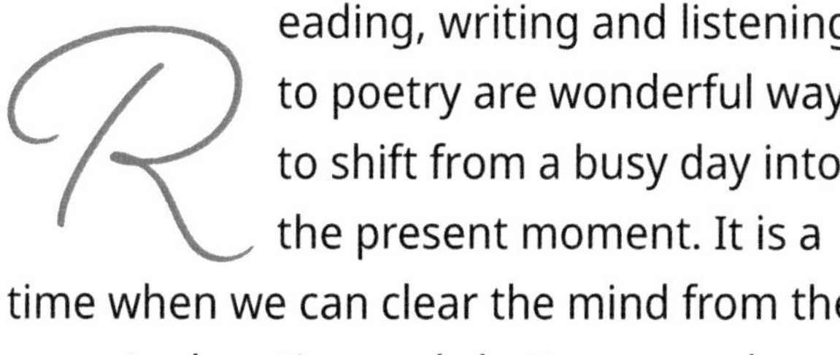

eading, writing and listening to poetry are wonderful ways to shift from a busy day into the present moment. It is a time when we can clear the mind from the perpetual motion and chatter around us.

After reading Alberto Villoldo's book, *Courageous Dreaming*, I was inspired to start writing Japanese haiku poetry, which consists of 17 syllables in three unrhymed lines of five, seven, and five syllables, often describing nature or a season.

In his book, Dr. Villoldo challenges his readers to tap into the present moment while observing nature—flowers, trees, birds, sunrises and sunsets—and then write a few poems.

I challenged myself to write two haiku poems each day for one month. I took 30 minutes a day to meditate and listen to my heart. Surprisingly, after only a few days of writing, I began to feel words flow through me. Now I keep a journal and pen nearby to write the words down as fast as they flow.

Writing poetry and journaling are perfect practices at any age, especially if your desire is to find peace and relaxation. These practices can lead to the development of greater creativity and inspiration to follow your dreams.

As you read each poem, imagine and feel the energy of the words. Perhaps you too will be inspired to write and take the journey into the present moment.

Love Is Life

Lifetimes

Time is all we have
Souls caught in eternity
Cycles of lifetimes

Freedom

Dive into the deep
Safe from unseen obstructions
Swimming with freedom

Waking

Gloom hangs on the edge
Thoughts of depression lurking
Suddenly sunshine

Live Now

Dreams of the future
Unperceivable thinking
Enjoy living now

Perspective

A new perspective
Change the level of vision
Accepting the truth

Moonlight

Tried to sleep last night
Rays of moonlight in her eyes
Love was on her mind

Haiku

Feel the flow of words
The energy of haiku
Five, seven and five

Keyboard

Touch the keys of life
Use the backspace to undo
Return and move on

Where Are You?

Where are you, my love?
Are you off in the sunset?
Let me come to you

All We Need

How love sustains us
There is nothing else to be
Love is all we need

Love is the Way

Love is the answer
There is no doubt about it
Try it and find out

Strong Emotions

What is this madness?
Emotions like a monsoon
Peace after the storm

Calmness

Low mist on the pond
Morning light exudes calmness
Reflective surface

Blankets of Love

Darkness all around
Swaddled in blankets of love
No reason to fear

Harmony

Love is all we need
Love removes all blockages
Love brings harmony

Thoughts

Thoughts are energy
Keep your thoughts pure and happy
Love is a good thought

Within the Heart

Expressions of love
Always dear within the heart
Silent like the night

Flowers

Soft petals of love
Colorful buds of laughter
Scented abundance

Light of the Heart

Reflections of love
Wondrous light of the heart
Shines gloriously

Compassion

Love is love but more
Compassion is compassion
Hate is hate but less

Peace on Earth

Born with compassion
Eternal love radiates
Hope for peace on Earth

Love

Consciousness of life
Profound impact on others
Love prevails for all

Look Around

Love is everywhere
Just look around to see it
You will be surprised

The Gift of Love

Love opens our hearts
The heart knows the gift of love
The heart knows kindness

Love is Energy

We are not alone
Love is always around us
Love is energy

Emptiness

Where did the love go?
Life is empty without love
Love lives in the heart

Love is Infinite

We are love like life
We are human like the earth
We are infinite

Miracles

Love for everyone
Imagine a peaceful world
Miracles happen

Life Is Beautiful

Life is magical
Life is full of mystery
Life is beautiful

Searching

Searching for answers
Keep moving and creating
They will be revealed

Solutions

Solutions to life
Stay positive and honest
Stay true to your heart

Without Purpose

The branches are bare
Living with nothing to show
Life without purpose

Life

Life is about growth
Learning, coping, forgiving
Most of all—loving

Forgiveness

Sometimes life can hurt
Try to forgive and let go
Look to the bright side

Treasures

The garden of life
Pathways and scented flowers
Uplifting treasures

Joy of Living

Life on Mother Earth
Listen to the wind and surf
Smell the air and wood

Happiness

Finding happiness
Walk through a field of poppies
Feel the earth rejoice!

Transformation

Death is a rebirth
Progressive transformation
We are going home

Friends

Someone to listen
Looking out for each other
That's what friends are for

Footprints

Fresh garden footprints
A stroll in the morning light
Inhale pristine air

Smiles

Echoes of laughter
Bright smiles on children playing
Sounds of happiness

The Garden Gate

A mission of love
Walk through the garden of peace
A spiritual place

The Light

Can you see the light?
Close your eyes and see it shine
It will guide you home

Change

In the waves of change
Trust spirit to keep you safe
Follow the current

Love Song

Sing a song of love
Let your heart feel the rhythm
And beat to each word

Golden Bridge

The bridge made of gold
Dimensions linked to spirit
A gateway for love

Fear

Strange feelings lurking
Energy of emotions
Sensing one is near

Hurt

Hurting from within
Feeling one another's pain
Wanting it to stop

Sound of Energy

Energy through sound
Music takes away the fear
Safe within the notes

The Truth

The truth is out there
It will be revealed in time
Only patience now

Answers

Searching for answers
Not sure where to start looking
Is the truth hiding?

Unfinished Work

Our task is not done
The universe will find us
We have work to do

Guardian Angel

An angel above
Guiding us in the darkness
Showing us the light

Mood Swings

Feeling rejected
Crying without knowing why
Then a burst of joy

Betrayal

Drowning in sadness
More deceit than she can take
Hope is always there

Journey

The ship has set sail
The journey of a lifetime
No jumping allowed

Ballerina

She walks on her toes
Touching the ground so gently
Lightness overflows

A Face

A stain on the wall
Draws people to stare at it
A face in the shape

Books

Lots of books to read
Pages and pages of words
Full of make-believe

Hidden Key

No one knows her dreams
The secrets within her heart
The key is hidden

Pathways

Lost and wandering
Searching for answers to life
Pathways through the trees

Heaven is Within

A hand reaches out
Sunlight passes through the soul
Heaven is within

Hope and Faith

Love is powerful
Hope and faith are essential
Life everlasting

Insecure

Undoubtably strong
A master at what she does
Without confidence

Courage

Courage to take off
Into the space beyond Earth
Feel your heart soaring

Caution

Her heart was open
Yellow rays of light burning
Cautiously moving

Bliss

A rainbow of love
Feel the lightness in your heart
Let the colors burst

Concealed

Regret, shame and guilt
Her heart broke a thousand times
Hiding in darkness

Blade

A sudden sharp stab
When does the pain go away?
Remove the dagger

Hearts and Souls

Souls come in all forms
Hearts and souls lost in the clouds
Waiting for the light

Now

There is no future
Caught in the middle of space
Everything is now

Lost Souls

Souls are everywhere
Wondering relentlessly
Only to be saved

Faith

Faith is having trust
God's hands hold our divine love
Life flowing with joy

♡

Letting Go

Losing a loved one
Holding on, not letting go
A soul's energy

Death

Floating and drifting
Leaving everything behind
Moving toward the light

♡

Going Within

Selfish pride takes hold
The shadow of the ego
Release, go within

Darkness

Dark clouds surround her
Patiently waiting for light
Her heart crying out

Breathe

Hold the moment dear
Exhale to release the past
Freedom is waiting

Meditation

An eye in darkness
Changing its form constantly
Light moving within

Sadness

Endless tears of pain
Robbing our life's source of love
Heaviness within

Choices

Forces of nature
On the gateway to our souls
Choices to be made

Feeling Words

Words felt through the heart
Each with a new vibration
Telling a story

Honesty

Deep within her heart
The universe is waiting
Discover the truth

Rebirth

Stepping into light
Rebirth is remembering
A new world awakes

Know Yourself

You know who you are
Search within to find yourself
Let your heart guide you

Mesmerized

Motionless water
A journey into the soul
No longer shallow

Emerge

A seed emerges
See the flower grow within
Be the flower now

Rose Garden

Roses bloom with grace
A garden thrives in our hearts
Overflowing bliss

Contemplation

Cut off from the world
Only to be found adrift
Floating on a cloud

Walking with Angels

Alone on the path
Kissing the earth with blessings
Lies proof of angels

How to Walk

Mindfully walking
Planting a kiss with each step
The earth rejoices

The Message

Silently knowing
A feather among the twigs
A sign from above

Reflecting Light

Gem-colored lights flash
Reflecting off the crystal
Rainbow shadows left

Twin Souls

Two souls in one thought
Healing each other with joy
Bridged in consciousness

The Light Within

Light comes pouring in
A door opens from within
Feeling of oneness

Green

The color of green
Exudes love and compassion
Use liberally

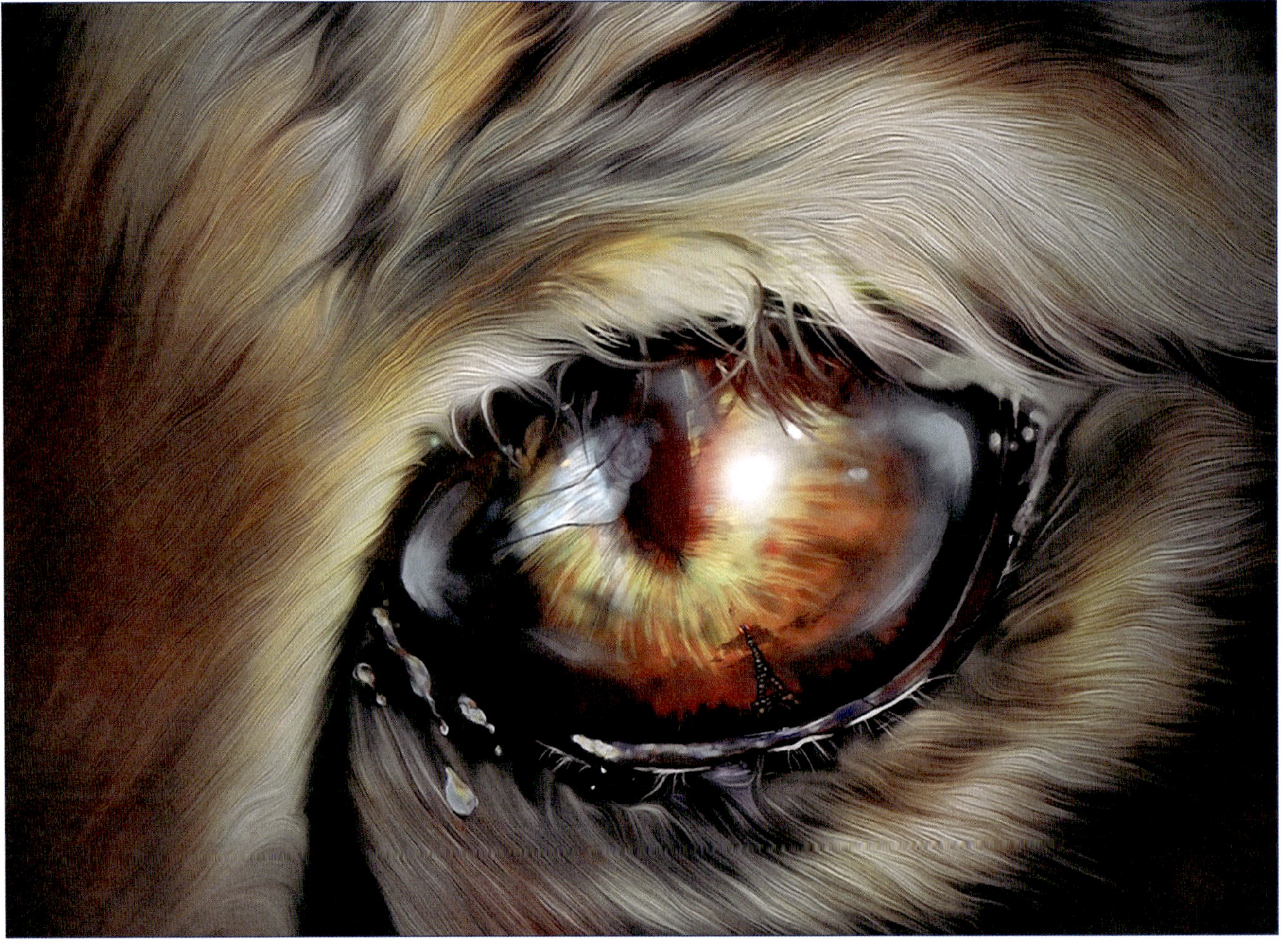

Eyes of Love

Heartfelt words spoken
There is nothing more to say
Only eyes of love

Just Love Her

Hopelessly falling
Just tell her that you love her
While she is living

Waves of Affection

Against all beliefs
Surging waves of affection
Beyond acceptance

Messages of Love

Knowing that feeling
Anticipates desire
Hearts beating faster

Another Day

Missing him deeply
It was just the other day
She saw him smiling

Heaven Rejoices

A rainbow of light
Shines down on the earth's surface
Heavenly souls cheer

Energy of Love

Through his eyes she sees
Bold colors of the sunset
Drawing her closer

Living in the Present

Living in the now
Shadows made in the sunset
Patiently waiting

Joyfulness

Orange blazing sunlight
Pink-filled clouds bursting with joy
Perfect alignment

Cycling

Through the winding road
Glimpses of flowers and trees
Passing by swiftly

Reflections

Crystal morning dew
Streaks of golden energy
Reflections of life

Mountain Biking

Wheels spinning around
Low gear to climb the mountain
Can't go back, push on

Nature and Creatures

Snowfall

Snow-covered mountains
Heavy clouds looming above
More snow will soon fall

Snowflakes

White snowflakes falling
Cold, windy air gusting through
Snow-covered treetops

Sounds of Dusk

Feel the evening breeze
Listen to the sounds of dusk
Soon it will be night

Angel Snowflakes

From heaven to earth
Glimmering snowflakes falling
Angels among us

Night Sounds

Sounds in the distance
Echoing through the night air
Footsteps approaching

End of the Day

Sunset in the west
Fades into the horizon
Where did the day go?

Sunshine on a Dark Day

A glimpse of sunlight
Breaks the darkness of the sky
Clouds drifting apart

Sunrise

A cold winter's dawn
Light beams from the horizon
Wake up, everyone!

Squall

A flash of lightning
A storm of great magnitude
A thunderous roar

A Mother's Love

Silent nurturing
Warm, caring, enveloping
Protector of love

The Bay

Liquid turquoise drops
Filling a bay of water
Saltwater crystals

The Beach

White sandy beaches
Bright multicolored shelters
Sun-golden lovers

Owl

Two eyes wide open
Fully focused on the prey
Every moment counts

Reptile

Innate precision
Slight ripples on the surface
Jumps for the reward

Lizard

The chameleon shifts
Changing colors as it moves
Cautiously but fast

Mammoth

Thick skin, tender heart
A herd of many members
Greatness in stature

Honeybee

Moving through the air
A reverberating hum
Scooping up pollen

Waiting

Stillness in the air
Silence looms before the storm
Anticipation

Needing Love

Barely hanging on
The heartbeat of magnolia
Love is required

Lost

Seemingly lost ant
Scurries to locate its nest
Treasures on its back

Morning Vibrations

Sounds of the morning
Birds transmitting vibrations
Some squawk, others sing

The Ocean Calls

The ocean calls her
Powerful waves pound the beach
Pulling her closer

Dawn's Light

Motionless beauty
In dawn's light appears
Amidst sand and time

The Wave

Feel the water pull back
It rises like an angry bear
Then crashes downward

Restoration

Healing salt water
Cleanse my soul of all my sins
Restore my spirit

Earth

A wonderous place to be
Between the moon and the sun
Planetary bliss

A Storm

Dark clouds passing by
Sounds of drums and flashing light
Animals hiding

Octopus

Eight long tentacles
Probing and grasping its prey
Flowing skillfully

Lanternfish

Swimming with sonar
Darkness at the deepest depths
Cautionary life

Mermaid's Love

A mermaid's true love
Her soul mate's heart beckoning
Vibrates through the waves

Instincts

The jaguar leaps
Takes the risk for survival
Holds on to the end

Mermaids

Mystical voyage
Virgin underwater world
Deep among mermaids

Looming Fog

Fog looms in silence
Forces of the universe
Gently passes by

Fog

Fog blankets the ridge
Looks like snow-covered mountains
Gently moves inland

Hawk

Razor-sharp talons
Equal power of a vice
Stretched out for the kill

Breeze

Serene ocean breeze
Tickles the leaves of the trees
Doesn't stop moving

Seashore

Tiny grains of sand
Beneath my feet as I walk
Along the seashore

Sunset

Rays of golden light
A spectacular display
Fades into abyss

Ocean

Ocean waves crashing
The formation of rocks weep
How much can they take?

Sand Dollars

Sand dollars glisten
Scattered along the wave line
Hoping to be saved

Primal Love

Safe in mother's arms
Dangling from a tree limb
A young monkey's life

A Trail of Seashells

Footprints in the sand
A trail of tiny seashells
Salt air and seaweed

Butterfly Effect

A butterfly's touch
Ripples on the still water
Sends motion outward

Morning Song

Wake up, pretty bird
Little robin in the tree
Sing a happy song

Dragonfly

Darting back and forth
Sunlight glitters on its wings
Golden fantasies

Summer

The ceiling fan hums
Birds singing their morning songs
Awaking heartbeat

The Hunt

The hawk flies above
A rabbit stands motionless
Unable to run

Seagull Soars

The seagull soars high
Watches the evening sunset
Gliding from above

Autumn

Transforming season
Falling from security
Dying gracefully

Roots

Roots penetrating
Groundbreaking and making room
Anchors a tower

Lessons

Learning to let go
The heart feels tremendous pain
Lessons for the soul

Sun Rays

Gentle rain comes down
Sunshine breaks through the dark clouds
The air is clear now

The Turtle

The turtle withdraws
Protected by its hard shell
Plays games with its prey

The Catch

Lurking in the sea
Waiting for the right moment
Snatched in just a flash

The Flight

The owl sees at night
A full moon glows for the flight
Nature is calling

Motionless Fear

Stillness on the branch
A slight movement is fatal
Motionless with fear

The Majestic Eagle

Perched high on a branch
Sits the majestic eagle
Spirit guardian

The Eagle Soars

Soaring through the sky
The eagle spies its kingdom
Large wings span above

Night Flight

Glides through the forest
Daring swoop to catch its prey
Stealth flight in the night

Strong Wind

Strong are the tree roots
Branches swaying in the wind
Holding on tightly

Power

Pure crystal water
Flowing freely with power
This is energy

Waterfall

Sound of rain falling
Water flows over the ground
Heads down the river

Earth Consciousness

Guests on a planet
Growing seeds of mindfulness
Conscious light beings

Hidden Hearts

Hearts of trees hidden
A treasure deeply within
Alive and growing

Flying

Watching birds fly by
Gracefully past my window
What's it like to fly?

Listen and Connect

Walking in nature
Connect to the earth and trees
Listen to the breeze

Being Ready

Crows on the rooftop
Mindfully watching the sky
Ready to take flight

Timing

Killer whales team up
Magnificent harmony
Essence of timing

New Beginnings

A double rainbow
Colors stretched across the sky
Brings new beginnings

Lotus Flower

Mud-covered petals
Rising up towards the sun
A new day is born

Rainbows

Light up your rainbow
A rainbow is within you
Become enlightened

Peace

The barefoot rabbit
A burrow for a safe home
Huddling for peace

Universe

Gaze out into space
The universe is open
Feel its energy

Shooting Stars

Dark night full of stars
Bright lights glow in the black sky
Suddenly one falls

Silence

Listen to silence
The sounds of everyday life
Hear the earth moving

Passage

Trunks form a tunnel
Heavy branches with green leaves
Provide the passage

Made in the USA
Monee, IL
19 February 2020

22005812R00064